The
Earth and
its Moon

Chris Oxlade

First published in Great Britain in 2007
by Wayland, an imprint of Hachette Children's Books
Reprinted in 2008

This paperback edition published in 2009 by
Wayland

Hachette Children's Books
338 Euston Road, London NW1 3BH
www.hachette.co.uk

Editor: Nicola Edwards
Designer: Tim Mayer
Consultant: Ian Graham

British Library Cataloguing in Publication Data
Oxlade, Chris
   Earth and its moon. - (Earth and space)
   1. Moon - Juvenile literature 2. Earth - Juvenile
   literature
   Title
   523.3

ISBN: 9780750247757

Cover: The Earth and its Moon are partners in space,
but they are two very different worlds.

Photo credits: James L. Amos/Corbis 23c. Stuart
Baines/Ecoscene: 17t, 17b, 37t. Andrew
Brown/Ecoscene: 18, 19. Lloyd Cuff/Corbis; 9.
Christian Darkin/SPL: 22. ESA: 24b.
ESA/CNES/ARIANESPACE-Service Optique CSG: 40.
Macduff Everton/Corbis: 14. Chinch
Gryniewicz/Ecoscene: 27. GSFC/NASA: 13t, 15t. F.
Hasler, M. Jentoff-Nilsen, H. Pierce, K. Palaniappan &
M. Manyin/GSFC/NASA: 10. Andy Hibbert/Ecoscene:
23b. HSTI/NASA: 20. George H. Huey/Corbis: 11.
JPL/NASA: 1, 4, 5, 32, 41. JSC/NASA: 28, 29, 30, 45.
Frank Lukassek/zefa/Corbis: 34. David Malin
Images/Anglo-Australian Observatory: 7. John & Lisa
Merrill/Corbis: 39. NASA: 6, 35. NASA/SPL: 16, 33t,
44. Graham Neden/Corbis: 12. Patrick
Pleul/epa/Corbis: 36. Jose Fuste Raga/Corbis: 21.
Detlev van Ravenswaay/SPL: 31. Roger
Ressmeyer/Corbis: 38. Reuters/Corbis: 8, 25c.
Ria/Novosti/SPL: 33b. Erik Schaffer/Ecoscene: 25.
Superstock: front cover. © Joe Tucciarone: 26. Ralph
White/ Corbis: 43. Jim Winkley/Ecoscene: 42.

Every attempt has been made to clear copyright.
Should there be any inadvertent omission please
apply to the publisher for rectification.

Contents

Earth and its Moon

Our Earth seems an enormous place to us. But it is just a small member of a whole family of planets. Together with the Sun, moons and other objects in space, these planets make up our Solar System. The Moon is the Earth's companion in space.

The planets

There are eight planets in our Solar System. The four planets nearest the Sun (Mercury, Venus, Earth and Mars: the inner planets) are rocky worlds with solid surfaces. The other four (Jupiter, Saturn, Uranus and Neptune) are huge balls of gas. They are known as the gas giants. Pluto, a small, icy body beyond Neptune, was classed as a planet until 2006, when experts at the International Astronomical Union decided to downgrade it to a 'dwarf planet'.

Earth's special nature

Earth is largest of the inner planets. It is the only place in the Solar System where there is liquid water on the surface, and where there is life. Astronomers have found planets around other stars, too, but so far, none like the Earth. Earth's blue oceans and green vegetation make it look very different to the other planets. We know it as the 'Blue Planet'.

From top to bottom, the planets (not to scale) are Mercury, Venus, Earth, Mars, Jupiter, Saturn, Uranus and Neptune.

The Moon

The Moon is the only natural object that orbits (moves around) the Earth. It is about one third the width of the Earth, and approximately 385,000 kilometres away. It is much larger than most of the moons in the Solar System. Some astronomers think of the Earth and Moon as a double planet. The Moon is a very different world to the Earth. It is covered with craters and dark regions called seas. There is no liquid water here, no atmosphere, and no life.

How do we know?

Walking on the Moon

The Moon is the only object (apart from the Earth) that humans have visited. American astronauts flew a series of missions to the Moon in Apollo craft, starting in 1969. The astronauts carried out experiments and brought back samples of Moon rock. The last visit was in 1972. Nobody has been to the Moon since, mainly because the cost is enormous.

The Earth and Moon are partners in space, but they are two very different worlds.

Moving Through Space

The Earth moves around the Sun in a path called an orbit, always staying about 150 million kilometres from the Sun. The orbit is the shape of a slightly squashed circle. The Moon orbits the Earth, remaining about 385,000 kilometres away from it.

Spinning worlds

The Earth and Moon spin round as they move along their orbits. The Earth spins round its axis, which is an imaginary line through the Earth. The Earth's poles are where this line sticks through the surface. The Earth's spin causes night and day to happen. As part of the world faces the Sun, it has day. As it faces away from the Sun, it is in the Earth's shadow and has night. The Earth completes one spin every day.

The Earth's spin also makes the Sun, Moon and stars appear to move across the sky as the day and night pass by. They don't really move. The Earth's spin means that you move in a giant circle once a day. It is like sitting on a spinning roundabout and seeing the playground it's in seem to move around you.

One side of the Earth lit by the Sun, seen from the Moon as it orbits the Earth.

The Moon also spins as it orbits the Earth. But it spins very slowly compared to the Earth. In fact, it completes exactly one spin during each orbit. This means that the same side of the Moon faces the Earth all the time.

SPACE DATA

Earth and Moon

Distance from Earth to Sun:	149.6 million km
Distance from Earth to Moon:	384,400 km
Earth: time for one spin:	23 hours, 56 minutes
Moon: time for one spin:	27.3 Earth days
Earth year:	365.26 days
Lunar month:	29.5 Earth days

This photograph was taken over several hours. The lines are star trails made by the Earth's spin.

Days, months and years

The movements of the Earth and Moon give us days, years and months. A day is the time it takes the Earth to complete one spin. A year is the time it takes the Earth to complete one orbit of the Sun. A lunar month is the time between one New Moon and the next.

Gravity

The force of gravity keeps the Earth and Moon in orbit. Gravity attracts the Earth to the Sun, and the Moon to the Earth. It acts like a string, stopping the Earth and Moon from flying off into space, and making them move in a circle. At the same time, because the Earth and Moon are moving along their orbits, they do not fall towards the Sun or Earth.

Earth's Structure

The Earth is a giant ball of rock. If you could dig a hole straight down to the centre of the Earth, you would find four different layers of rock. The surface we stand on is solid, but not many kilometres under our feet there is runny, partly molten rock. This makes the surface rocks move about, and causes earthquakes and volcanoes.

Layers of the Earth

The first layer of the Earth is the crust. Under the Earth's continents, the crust is 35 kilometres thick on average. But it is only a few kilometres thick under the oceans. Under the crust is a layer of rock nearly 3,000 kilometres thick, called the mantle. It makes up about three-quarters of the Earth. Just under the crust, the mantle is so hot that its rock is partly molten.

Under the mantle is the Earth's core, which is about 7,000 kilometres across. The core is made mostly of iron. It has two layers, a solid inner core and a molten outer core.

Powerful seismic waves travelling across the Earth's surface can cause damage such as this, in Kobe, Japan.

How do we know?
Seismic waves

A seismic wave is a wave that moves through the Earth's rock. Seismic waves are caused by earthquakes. The waves spread through the Earth from where the earthquake happens. They bounce or change direction when they hit a boundary between different layers of rock. Studying where waves arrive at the Earth's surface after earthquakes has allowed geologists to detect the layers deep inside the Earth.

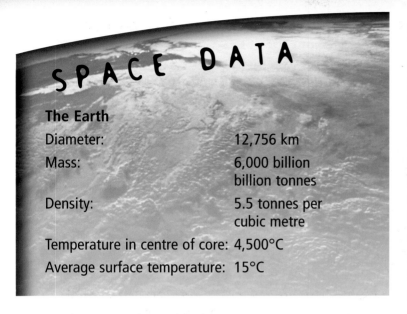

This giant crack is called the San Andreas fault. It is where two tectonic plates meet in California, USA.

A cracked crust

The Earth's crust is cracked into giant pieces called tectonic plates. Slow moving molten rock in the mantle makes the plates move very slowly. This movement is called continental drift. In some places the edges of the plates are moving apart. In others they slide past each other. Sometimes the edges of plates collide with each other. Earthquakes happen when the moving plates become jammed and then move suddenly. As far as we know, the Earth is the only planet with these tectonic plates.

Earth's Surface

From space the Earth looks very different from the other planets in the Solar System. Astronauts are the only people lucky enough to see Earth from space. From the photographs they send back we can see a surface that is made up of blue water, green vegetation, brown rock and soil, and white ice.

Water

Two-thirds of the Earth's surface is covered with oceans. The largest ocean, the Pacific, covers nearly half of the globe. The oceans are thousands of metres deep. They contain 97 per cent of all the Earth's water. One per cent of the water is in lakes and rivers, and in underground rocks. The other 2 per cent is in the form of ice, in mountain glaciers, and in thick ice sheets at the poles.

Land masses

Land covers about a third of the Earth's surface. The landscape is made up of a wide variety of features, such as mountain ranges and flat plains. Mountain ranges such as the Himalayas and Andes are mostly at the boundaries between the tectonic plates, where the colliding plates force up the surface rocks.

The Earth is dominated by its oceans. It is often described as looking like a giant blue marble.

Earth Facts

Earth's features

● The highest point on the Earth's surface is the summit of Mount Everest, at 8,848 metres above sea level.

● The lowest point on Earth is the bottom of the Marianas Trench, in the Pacific Ocean, at 10,924 metres below sea level.

Earth has hundreds of active volcanoes, which also build mountains. Most volcanoes are at the plate boundaries, where molten rock pushes its way to the surface.

Water features

The Earth has deep canyons and valleys that have been cut by flowing rivers and glaciers. Alongside the rivers are wide plains, and at their ends, where they meet the sea, are deltas. River basins are huge areas that are drained by a system of rivers. At the coasts are cliffs and beaches.

Islands

The Grand Canyon in Arizona, USA, was cut over millions of years by the flowing water of the Colorado River.

Dotted in the oceans are islands. Some islands are actually part of the continents. The land is separated from the rest of the continent when the sea level rises. Islands far out in the oceans, such as the Hawaiian Islands, are normally the tops of giant undersea volcanoes.

The Atmosphere

The atmosphere is a layer of air that surrounds the Earth. It is very thin compared to Earth, like the skin on an apple. Moving upwards, the atmosphere gradually gets thinner and thinner until it runs out a few hundred kilometres up.

Gases of the atmosphere

The main two gases in atmosphere are nitrogen and oxygen, the gas we need to breathe. Nitrogen makes up 78 per cent of the air, and oxygen 20 per cent. The remaining 2 per cent is made up of many different gases, including carbon dioxide. There is always some water vapour in the atmosphere, too. A special form of oxygen, called ozone, exists in the upper atmosphere. The ozone layer stops much of the harmful ultraviolet radiation that comes from the Sun from reaching the surface.

Weather balloons carry instruments up into the atmosphere to measure things such as temperature and pressure at different altitudes.

A satellite image showing the 'ozone hole' over the Antarctic.

The greenhouse effect

The Earth's atmosphere acts like a blanket for the Earth. Heat comes through the atmosphere from the Sun, and warms the surface. The Earth's surface gives off heat. Some gases in the atmosphere trap this heat, warming the atmosphere. The gases that trap most heat are carbon dioxide and methane. This effect is called the greenhouse effect because glass in a greenhouse traps heat in a similar way.

Threats to the atmosphere

In the last two hundred years, we have added gases to the atmosphere that are changing how the atmosphere works. For example, chemicals called CFCs, used in fridges and freezers, have caused a hole in the ozone layer. Carbon dioxide from burning fuels is increasing the greenhouse effect, making the atmosphere warmer. This is known as global warming. Most scientists agree that global warming is changing the world's climates.

How do we know?
Measuring the atmosphere

We know about the atmosphere from measurements and observations from the Earth and from space. Measurements of the atmosphere, such as the air pressure, temperature and concentration of different gases, are taken by aircraft and by instruments carried by weather balloons. Satellites observe the atmosphere from above.

Earth's Weather

The weather that happens on Earth is driven by the Sun. The Sun's heat warms the Earth's surface, and the warm surface heats the air above it. This heat makes winds blow and clouds form, and causes giant swirling weather systems that are visible from space.

Rising and falling air

The Sun's heat warms some parts of the Earth's surface more than others. The surface is heated more where the Sun shines from high in the sky, and less where the Sun's rays hit at a low angle. Bare soil also heats up more than land covered with plants, and the oceans.

Where the surface is warmed up, it heats the air above it. This makes the air expand. It becomes less dense and floats upwards. Cooler air flows in sideways to replace it. This moving air creates winds. As the air moves across the Earth's surface, the spinning of the Earth underneath it makes the winds swirl round to form weather systems. The moving air spreads heat over the Earth's surface.

Here, humid air has been heated by warm land and risen. Its water vapour has formed clouds.

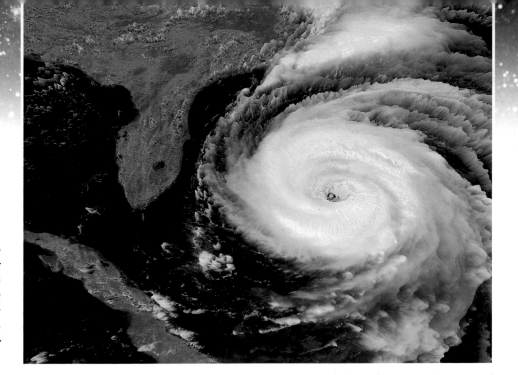

In some parts of the world, masses of giant thunderstorms form into damaging weather systems called hurricanes (also known as cyclones or typhoons).

Clouds and rain

The heat from the Sun also warms the water in the oceans and in the soil. Some of the water evaporates, turning into a gas called water vapour. This warm, humid air rises upwards. As it does, it cools. This makes the water vapour condense. It turns to tiny drops of water. Billions of these drops form clouds. If the drops become large enough, they fall back to the surface as rain.

The water cycle

When rain falls onto the ground, some soaks in. The rest runs across the surface and collects in streams and rivers. The water in the rivers flows down to the sea. Some of it then evaporates to form new clouds and rain. Some of the water in the soil and on the ground evaporates and goes back into the air, too. So water circulates between the oceans, the atmosphere and the land. This is called the water cycle. It carries water across the land masses, allowing life to survive on Earth.

SPACE DATA

Extreme weather records

Highest temperature:	58°C (Libya)
Lowest temperature:	-89°C (Antarctica)
Fastest wind:	371 km/h (Mount Washington, USA)
Heaviest rain:	38.1 mm in a minute (Guadeloupe)

Climates and Seasons

The pattern of weather a place on Earth has is called a climate. Different places on the Earth have different climates. In some places it is freezing cold all year round. In others it is hot and rainy all year. Many places have seasons, with different weather at different times of year.

Climate zones

The climate that a place has depends mainly on how far it is from the equator (an imaginary line around the middle of the Earth). Close to the equator the Sun shines from high overhead all year. There is also high rainfall most of the year. This is a tropical climate. Close to the Earth's poles the Sun's rays hit at a very low angle. The snow and ice also reflect the heat. So here it is extremely cold all year round. This is called a polar climate. Between the equator and the poles, many places have cool winters and warm summers. This is a temperate climate. In some places on Earth it is very dry all year. This is an arid climate. The climate a place has also depends on how close it is to the oceans, and how high up it is.

The sort of vegetation in a place is closely linked to the climate. In polar climates it is too cold for plants to grow, and the ground is covered with snow and ice. In very arid climates it is too dry, and so there are brown deserts. In tropical climates there is dense rainforest. And in temperate climates there are forests of deciduous and coniferous trees.

A map of daytime temperatures shows that the equator is heated more than the polar regions.

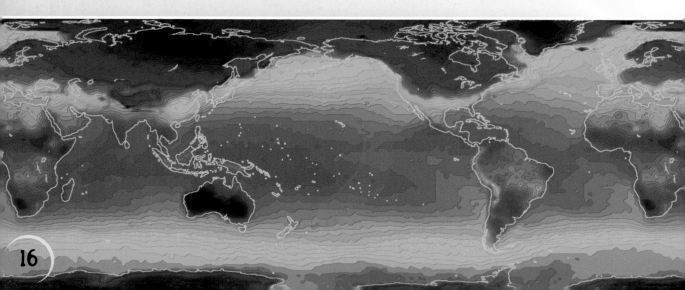

What causes seasons

Seasons happen because the Earth's axis is tilted over to one side. A place has summer when the pole it is nearest to is tilted towards the Sun. On the opposite side of the orbit, this pole is tilted away from the Sun. Then it gets less heat, and it is winter. When it is summer in the northern hemisphere, it is winter in the southern hemisphere, and vice versa. The tilt also means that there are more hours of sunshine in summer than in winter. In mid-summer, places near the Earth's poles have daylight 24 hours a day. In mid-winter, they have 24 hours of darkness.

The same wood in summer and winter in a temperate part of the world.

Earth Facts

Extreme climates

● The Atacama Desert in Chile is the driest place on Earth. Some areas of the Atacama have had no rain for 400 years.

● The wettest place on Earth is Maghalaya State in northeast India, where nearly 12 metres of rain fall every year.

Life on Earth

As far as we know, the Earth is the only place in the Solar System where there is life. The Earth supports a staggering variety of life, from microscopic bacteria to towering trees and giant whales.

Water and air

Life can only exist on Earth because there is liquid water. Animals also rely on oxygen in the atmosphere to breathe. Without water and the atmosphere, the Earth would be as dry and lifeless as the Moon. Earth has liquid water because it is just the right distance from the Sun. If it were closer to the Sun, the water would boil away. If it were further away from the Sun, the water would be frozen.

The biosphere

The biosphere is made up of all the places on Earth where life exists. It includes the ocean bottoms to mountain summits, rivers and lakes, soil, the surface and the atmosphere.

Cacti are adapted to live in the desert, where they may get no water for months on end.

Life thrives in the world's rainforests, where there is plenty of sunshine and rainfall.

The oceans are vast compared to the land. They make up 97 per cent of the biosphere. The biosphere is as big as it is because forms of life have adapted to survive in extreme conditions, such as those in the polar ice caps and the ocean depths.

Energy for life

All the energy needed for animals and plants to grow and live comes from the Sun. Plants use energy in sunlight to grow. They are at the bottom of the food chain. Some animals eat the plants as food. Other animals eat these animals and are in turn eaten by others.

The origins of life

So how do scientists think that life on Earth began? The Earth was formed about 4,600 million years ago. About 4,000 million years ago, the Earth looked very different from how it does today. It was covered in volcanoes that brought a mixture of chemicals to the surface during eruptions. The chemicals mixed with water, forming pools. The chemicals in the pools reacted together to form the complex chemicals that are the building blocks of life. These grouped together to form the very first, very simple forms of life.

Earth Facts

Life facts

● The chemical reactions that created the complex chemicals needed for life may have been set off by lightning strikes.

● None of the Earth's early forms of life exists today. In fact, 99 per cent of all the life forms that have ever lived are extinct.

Formation of the Earth

The Earth was formed about 4,600 million years ago. This was at the same time that the Sun and other planets were formed too. The Earth began its life as a ball of hot rock with a molten surface.

A nebula far out in space. It may form new solar systems in the distant future.

Birth of the Solar System

The whole of our Solar System formed from part of a vast cloud of gas and dust called a nebula. About 5 billion years ago, gravity made the gas and dust very slowly clump together, and begin to spin. Then gravity made it collapse more quickly to form an extremely dense ball of material. Intense heat and pressure in the centre of the ball started nuclear reactions. Energy from the reactions produced heat and light, so the ball began to shine. This was our Sun.

Planetesimals and planets

We still don't really understand how the planets formed, but it was probably something like this. There was a spinning disc of material left over after the Sun formed. This was made up of gas, dust and small grains of rock. When bits of the rock and dust collided, they stuck together. Very slowly, gravity pulled these larger pieces of rock together. Over thousands of years boulders formed, which are known as planetesimals. They were the building blocks of the planets. Eventually, gravity pulled the planetesimals together to form the Earth and other planets.

Overall it took 100 million years for the Earth and other planets to form. The material left over from the formation of the Sun also formed the moons around the planets, and all the other bits of the Solar System, such as asteroids and comets.

The early Earth

The Earth began its life with a molten surface. The surface gradually cooled as heat escaped into space. Eventually it became solid. The space between the planets was filled with lumps of rock that bombarded their surfaces, smashing holes in them. These massive collisions created heat that kept the Earth's surface hot. A really huge collision probably smashed off a piece of Earth, forming the Moon (see pages 26-27). Gradually the bombardment subsided. But the surface was still covered in volcanoes that spewed lava over the surface. You can find out how the Earth has changed since on page 22.

All the Earth's rocks, such as these in Yosemite National Park in the USA, are formed from materials that came from a nebula.

Earth's Story

Earth was a very different place now than it was when it was formed 4,600 million years ago. Then there was no atmosphere, no oceans, no mountain ranges, no rivers, and no life. Over billions of years the Earth has transformed into the planet we know today.

The moving continents

Today the Earth's crust is made up of giant tectonic plates (see page 9). These may have formed more than 2 billion years ago. They have been slowly moving ever since. Hundreds of millions of years ago, the continents were in completely different places from where they are today. For example, about 400 million years ago, Africa was at the South Pole.

This is how the Earth looked about 250 million years ago. This 'supercontinent' is known as Pangaea.

Oceans and atmosphere

The water that now fills the Earth's oceans, lakes and rivers probably came from volcanoes. It came out as water vapour, then condensed in the air, forming clouds. Rain from the clouds gathered to form the oceans. Some of our water may have come from comets that collided with the Earth.

Chemicals from the eruptions also formed the atmosphere. At first it was made up of carbon dioxide, water vapour, nitrogen and other chemicals. There was no oxygen. The oxygen in today's atmosphere was given off by plants.

Life-changing events

The bombardment of rocks that hit the Earth in its early life has almost stopped, but not completely. Meteorites do still hit the Earth. In the past, large impacts have destroyed many species of animals and plants. A huge meteorite impact may have helped to kill off the dinosaurs.

Climate change

The world's climates have been changing for millions of years. For example, there have been periods of cold, called ice ages, when thick ice sheets covered much of the Earth. These changes took place over thousands or millions of years. Today, the temperature of the atmosphere is changing so fast that scientists think emissions from burning fuels is the cause (see page 13).

In the Earth's early life, the Earth would have been covered in hundreds of craters like this one in Arizona, USA.

How do we know?

Studying fossils

We know about the history of the Earth from its rocks. One way to tell the age of a piece of rock is to look at the fossils in it. Fossils are the remains of ancient plants and animals. If a rock contains a fossil of a particular plant or animal, geologists can tell how old it is because they know when the plant or animal lived.

A palaeontologist extracts a dinosaur fossil from some rock. Without fossils, we would not know that the dinosaurs ever existed.

The Changing Surface

The Earth's surface is still changing today. The tectonic plates are moving slowly, at a few centimetres a year. This movement builds up the landscape in places, and erosion wears it away again. These processes slowly change the surface, so features that were present millions of years ago no longer exist.

Lava flowing from volcanoes, such as this one in the Philippines, forms new rock on the Earth's surface.

Mountain building

The Earth's mountains are built up where the edges of tectonic plates collide into each other. This crumples the layers of rock at one or both edges, pushing up mountain ranges. For example, the Himalayas were created when the Indian plate collided with the Eurasian plate. Mountains are also built up by volcanoes. Others are formed when molten rock rises underground, pushing up the surface above.

How do we know?

Remote sensing

We can see how the Earth's surface is changing with the help of remote sensing satellites. The satellites take photographs, make three-dimensional maps and take measurements of the surface and atmosphere. Many satellites have been launched to monitor the changes that human activities are causing to the Earth, such as melting glaciers and the hole in the ozone layer (see page 13).

This photograph of Kazakhstan and the Caspian Sea was taken by the Envisat remote sensing satellite.

At coasts, the action of waves breaks up rocks, causing coastal erosion. In other places the coast is built up.

Erosion

As fast as new mountains are built up, they are worn down again by erosion. The rocks are broken up in different ways. Repeated heating and cooling in the day and night makes rocks crack. Ice forming in cracks also breaks up rocks. Rocks are worn away by loose rock particles blowing in the wind. They are also broken up when they are hit by particles carried along by flowing water, glaciers (slowly moving rivers of ice) and waves. Once rocks are broken up, they are carried away downhill by flowing water and the wind. The particles of rock are called sediment. The sediment is deposited where a river flows across flat plains, and at the sea. Over millions of years, whole mountain ranges are worn away and turned to layers of sediment.

The rock cycle

Old rocks are always being destroyed, and new rocks are continually being made. For example, old rocks are destroyed by erosion, and new rocks are made when molten rock flows from volcanoes, cools and solidifies. Sediment slowly forms new rocks when it becomes buried deep underground.

The Moon

The Moon is Earth's only natural satellite (a satellite is an object that orbits another object). The Moon looks very different from the Earth. It is covered with craters, it has no atmosphere or water, and no life. The Moon is kept in its orbit by gravity pulling the Earth and Moon together.

Near and far

The Moon spins on its axis very slowly compared to the Earth. It completes one spin every time it orbits the Earth, so that the same side of the Moon faces the Earth all the time. The Moon spins like this because Earth's gravity has locked one side of the Moon in place. We call this side of the Moon the near side. The opposite side of the Moon, called the far side, is always hidden from Earth. The only people who have seen the far side are the astronauts who have visited the Moon.

How the Moon formed

We know a lot about the Moon, but nobody is really sure how the Moon formed in the first place. Astronomers have suggested several theories.

This is what the collision that created the Moon may have looked like. Debris from the collision formed the Moon.

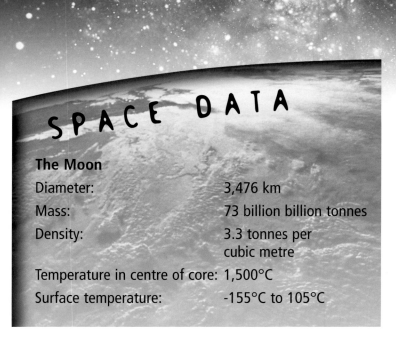

SPACE DATA

The Moon

Diameter:	3,476 km
Mass:	73 billion billion tonnes
Density:	3.3 tonnes per cubic metre
Temperature in centre of core:	1,500°C
Surface temperature:	-155°C to 105°C

One is that the Earth and Moon formed at the same time from the same cloud of rock and dust. Another is that the Moon drifted close to the Earth and was captured in its orbit by the Earth's gravity. But the most popular theory is that the Earth was hit by a huge body, perhaps as big as Mars. This threw huge amounts of rock into space, which came together to form the Moon.

Structure of the Moon

Like the Earth, the Moon has a crust, a mantle and a core. Unlike the Earth, there are no tectonic plates, and no volcanoes. This means that the Moon's surface does not change over time as the Earth's surface does. This is why craters that were made by meteorite impacts hundreds of millions of years ago are still visible. Part of the Moon's core may be molten. Movements of the rock here may cause 'moonquakes' that have been recorded by instruments on Moon's surface which were taken to the Moon by astronauts and lunar probes.

The Moon seen from Earth. This side of the Moon always faces the Earth.

Moon Rock

On Earth, new rocks are made and old rocks are destroyed all the time. This does not happen on the Moon. All the Moon's rock is at least 3,000 million years old. It was formed when the Moon cooled and crusted over.

Weathering on the Moon

The Moon's surface is covered with a thick layer of dust, rock fragments and boulders. This mixture is called regolith. It is formed as solid rock is broken up into dust by two types of weathering. The first is heat-cool weathering. This happens because the surface is heated to +105°C and cooled to −155°C as parts of the Moon move in and out of sunlight. It makes the rocks expand and contract, which cracks them apart. The second form of weathering is called 'space weathering'. This is caused by meteorite impacts that pulverise the rock. Most of the impacts are micrometeorites, less than 1 millimetre across, travelling at speeds up to 100,000 kilometres per hour.

The collisions that caused these hundreds of craters smashed the Moon's rock into dust.

An astronaut from the Apollo 17 mission uses an adjustable scoop to collect samples of rock from the Moon's surface.

How do we know?

Collecting Moon rock

We know a great deal about the Moon's rocks from examining the rock samples brought back to Earth by the astronauts of the Apollo missions. In total, astronauts from the six Apollo missions brought back 380 kg of Moon rock. In 1970 the Soviet probe *Luna 16* automatically collected a sample of Moon dust and sent it back to Earth in a rocket-powered capsule.

Light and dark rocks

From Earth we can see that the Moon's surface has light and dark areas. These areas are formed from two different types of rock. The lighter areas are made mainly from a light-coloured rock called anorthosite, and the darker areas are made from dark-coloured rock similar to basalt.

As the Moon's surface cooled, the anorthosite floated to the surface, cooled and solidified, forming the Moon's crust. This happened more than 4,000 million years ago. The darker, basalt-like rock was formed afterwards, when molten rock leaked through the crust and filled giant craters to form the Moon's seas. This happened between 4,000 million and 3,000 million years ago.

The Moon's Craters

The Moon's surface is littered with craters. They were formed by thousands of meteorites smashing into the Moon's surface at incredibly high speed. Most craters were formed more than 3.5 billion years ago. The craters are still there because there is no erosion on the Moon to wear the surface away.

Bowls and saucers

The Moon's craters exist in a wide range of sizes, from mini craters less than a metre across, to giant craters hundreds of kilometres across. There were even larger craters in the Moon's early life. Some of them have been flooded by lava to form the Moon's seas (see page 32). The biggest impacts cracked the surface, forming features such as scarps (steep steps in the landscape). In many places there are craters within craters, and in others, overlapping craters.

Craters are made up of a central bowl with a raised rim around the edge.

SPACE DATA

The Moon

Largest crater:	Bailly, diameter: 295 km
Deepest crater:	Newton, 8,850 metres from top of wall to floor
Brightest crater:	Aristarchus

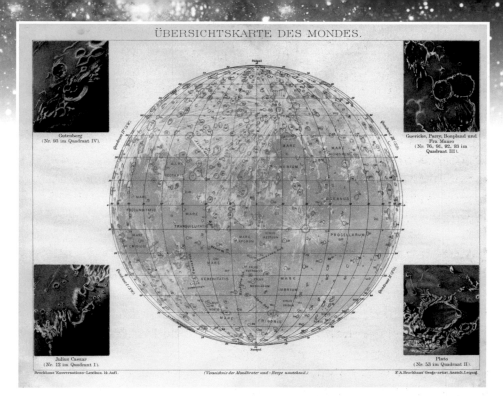

ÜBERSICHTSKARTE DES MONDES.

A map of the near side of the Moon. The craters are named after famous people, such as the philosopher, Plato, and Gutenberg, the inventor.

Small impacts create simple, shallow, bowl-shaped craters, up to a few kilometres across. The surface rocks are thrown up to form a wall around the crater. Medium-sized impacts affect layers of rock deeper in the crust. These layers bounce back to form a central peak in a flat-bottomed, saucer-shaped crater. Massive impacts create giant explosions that throw up rings of mountains around and inside the crater. Surface rock is thrown thousands of kilometres outwards.

Ray craters

A few of the Moon's craters are younger than the others. They were made by meteorites that hit the Moon after the bombardment in its early life died down. The material thrown outwards by the impacts can still be seen as rays spreading out from the craters.

Space facts

Crater theories

● Until the middle of last century, many astronomers thought that the Moon's craters were the tops of volcanoes.

● During a full moon, you can see three of the brightest ray craters, Tycho, Copernicus and Kepler.

More Surface Features

Craters are not the Moon's only features. The other main features are huge dark regions known as seas. The Moon also has huge mountain ranges and wide canyons.

Seas

The Moon's seas are not really seas, as there is no liquid water on the Moon. They were called seas because they looked like seas to early astronomers. They are actually giant, flat-bottomed basins. The seas are the result of meteorite impacts in the early history of the Moon. These impacts created vast craters. Later, the craters flooded with molten rock that leaked from under the crust. The impacts that created the larger seas were extremely powerful. For example, the crater that formed the Mare Imbrium was more than 1,000 kilometres across.

The large, dark grey patches are the Moon's seas. You can see them easily from Earth.

This photograph, taken during the Apollo 15 mission, shows Schroter's Valley on the Moon's surface.

Mountains and valleys

The Moon's mountains formed in a different way to the Earth's mountains. Like the craters and seas, the Moon's mountain ranges were formed by impacts. They are made up of the material thrown outwards by giant impacts. For example, the Montes Apenninus range runs along the edge of the Mare Imbrium, and was formed by the impact that created the sea. There are also some canyons on the Moon. These were not formed by water, but by flowing lava.

Near and far side

The near side and far side of the Moon are quite different. The far side has more craters than the near side, but is has only a few, very small seas. Astronomers do not yet understand why these differences exist.

How do we know?

Trips to the far side

Astronomers have studied the near side of the Moon for thousands of years, but we had no idea what the far side looked like until 1959. That was the year that a probe, *Luna 3*, first went into orbit around the Moon, and sent photographs back to Earth. The first people to see the far side were the astronauts of Apollo 8 in 1968, as the craft was tested for the Moon landings the following year.

The Luna 3 *probe*

Phases of the Moon

We see the Moon because light from the Sun bounces off it. The Sun lights only one side of the Moon. The Moon seems to change shape from day to day because we see different parts of this lit side as the Moon moves around its orbit. These shapes are called the phases of the Moon.

The changing Moon

A crescent Moon is seen just before and just after a New Moon.

When the Moon is on the opposite side of the Earth to the Sun, the Sun lights up the whole of the near side of the Moon. So we see a complete disc. This is called a Full Moon. When the Moon is on the same side of the Earth as the Sun, the Sun lights up the far side of the Moon. None of the near side is lit, so the Moon is dark. This is called a New Moon.

Between the New Moon and the Full Moon we see different amounts of the lit side. A few days after a New Moon we see a thin slice of Moon, called a crescent Moon. A few days later we can see half a Moon. A few days after this we see three-quarters of a Moon, called a gibbous Moon. Then we see the Full Moon. After the Full Moon, the Moon's lit part gradually gets smaller again, until we see the New Moon again. The whole process, between one New Moon and the next, on average takes 29.5 days. This is called a lunar month.

Tides

The gravitational pull of the Moon causes the tides in the oceans on Earth. The Moon pulls the water on the nearest side of the Earth into a bulge a few metres high. A bulge also forms on the opposite side of the Earth. The bulges stay still as the Earth spins underneath them. A place on Earth moves through two bulges a day, making the tide rise and fall twice a day. The Sun's gravity also affects the tides. The highest and lowest tides happen when the Sun and Moon are in line with each other, which is on the days of the New Moon and Full Moon.

This composite photograph shows the phases of the Moon from one New Moon to another.

Earth Fact

Highest tides

● The largest tidal range in the world happens in the Bay of Fundy, Canada. At high tide, sea level is 16 metres higher than at low tide.

Eclipses

A shadow forms where an object blocks out light. The Earth makes a shadow in space on the opposite side of the Earth to the Sun. The Moon makes a shadow, too. Sometimes the movements of the Earth, Moon and Sun bring them all into line. Then the Moon casts a shadow on the Earth, or the Earth casts a shadow on the Moon. These events are called eclipses.

Solar eclipses

A solar eclipse happens when the Moon casts a shadow on the Earth. The Moon's shadow is much smaller than the Earth, so it makes a dark spot on the Earth's surface. The shadow has a dark centre, called the umbra, and a lighter edge, called the penumbra. The Moon's movement along its orbit, and the Earth's spin make the shadow move across the surface.

When the dark central shadow moves over a place on the Earth's surface, people there see a total eclipse of the Sun. From the Earth, the Moon and Sun appear to be almost the same size, and during a total eclipse, the Moon just covers the Sun. Then it goes dark, like night, and the temperature drops. It takes a few minutes for the shadow to sweep past.

A partial eclipse happens when part of the Sun is blocked out by the Moon.

Total eclipses happen only every few years. Partial eclipses are more common. These happen when the outer, lighter shadow of the Moon passes over places on Earth. The Sun is not completely covered, but the Moon appears to take a bite out of it.

The Moon seen from the Earth during a lunar eclipse.
The top is still lit by the Sun.

Total eclipses of the Sun are useful events for astronomers. The Moon blocks out the brightness of the Sun's light, allowing them to study the Sun's outer atmosphere.

Never look directly at the Sun, with or without binoculars or a telescope, even during an eclipse. It could seriously damage your eyes.

Lunar eclipses

A lunar eclipse happens when the Earth casts a shadow on the Moon. It only happens when there is a full Moon, when the Earth is directly between the Sun and Moon. A lunar eclipse makes all or part of the Moon disappear in darkness.

SPACE DATA

Future total solar eclipses

Date	Where visible
August 2008	Canada, Greenland, Siberia, Mongolia, China
July 2009	India, Nepal, China, central Pacific
July 2010	South Pacific, Easter Island, Chile, Argentina

How we Observe the Earth and its Moon

Our knowledge of the Earth, Moon, and the rest of the Solar System, has come from making observations from Earth and from space, and from sending astronauts and spacecraft to explore space. You can find out about exploration on page 40.

Telescopes

The main way of observing the Moon (and other objects in space) from Earth is by using optical telescopes. An optical telescope makes distant objects appear larger, so that we can see more detail in the objects than we can see with the naked eye. Optical telescopes work by collecting light coming from an object and focusing it to form an image of the object. There are two main types of telescope. A refracting telescope uses a lens to collect and focus the light. A reflecting telescope uses a mirror instead. The larger the mirror or lens, the more light that can be collected, and the more detail that can be seen in an object. Most astronomers use reflecting telescopes because they give clearer images and because large mirrors are easier to make than large lenses.

The image made by a telescope's lens or mirror is viewed with an eyepiece, which works like a magnifying glass. Astronomers also use electronic detectors, like the chips in digital cameras, that record the image so that it can be viewed and processed by a computer.

These large binoculars are made up of two telescopes. They are excellent for studying the Moon.

Remote sensing

Much of what we know about the Earth has been learned by observations that scientists have made on the surface. But our knowledge has been widened by making observations from satellites above the Earth. From their orbits, these satellites can see a wide area of the Earth's surface. The satellites carry a wide variety of sensors. These sensors detect light and other forms of radiation, such as infra-red and ultra-violet coming from Earth, and send their data back to Earth by radio. Using satellites like this is called remote sensing. Remote sensing is used to study the atmosphere, the oceans and the land. For example, satellites measure the level of different gases in the atmosphere over the globe, the speed of ocean currents, and the type of vegetation on the surface.

Large optical telescopes are sited on mountain tops so that they are less likely to be affected by cloud cover.

Earth Facts

Telescope records

● The largest telescope mirrors in the world are in the twin Keck telescopes, in Hawaii. Each is 10 metres across.

● The latest research telescopes have mirrors that change shape all the time to remove the distortion of images caused by the Earth's atmosphere.

How we Explore the Earth and its Moon

Looking through telescopes can only tell us a certain amount about our Solar System. And it can't tell us anything about the places we can't see, such as the far side of the Moon. To find out more, we have to visit them, or send space probes to them, and that means going into space.

Getting into space

Space is only a few hundred kilometres away, but it is extremely hard to get there because of the Earth's gravity. If a spacecraft simply went straight up and then switched off its engines, it would fall straight back to Earth. Instead, spacecraft aim to go into orbit at high speed, a few hundred kilometres above the Earth. Their high speed means that they don't fall back to Earth, but circle it instead.

A rocket lifts off. About nine-tenths of its weight is made up of fuel for the engines.

The speed a spacecraft must reach to stay in orbit is 28,000 kilometres per hour. That's about thirty times as fast as a jet airliner. Any slower and the spacecraft would lose altitude again. Spacecraft need an enormous push to lift them into orbit and to reach orbital speed.

They need extremely powerful launch vehicles, such as rockets and space shuttles. Their rocket engines produce huge thrust and also work in space, where there is no air.

After a vertical lift off, a rocket gains height and then gradually tilts further to one side. When it reaches space, it is flying parallel to the Earth's surface.

Probes

Probes are unmanned spacecraft that visit other planets. To leave Earth's orbit and travel into the Solar System, a probe must travel even faster – at about 40,000 kilometres per hour. This allows it to escape Earth's gravity. Once the probes are up to this speed, they can switch off their engines. There is no air in space to slow them down again. Some probes are designed to orbit or land on other planets. They have to slow down again to drop into orbit or descend to the surface.

NASA's CloudSat experimental satellite is able to observe clouds from space and send back information about precipitation. CloudSat was carried into orbit in 2006 by a Delta II rocket.

Manned space flights

Sending astronauts out into the Solar System is far more difficult than sending probes. The astronauts have to take everything they need with them, including air and water. Their spacecraft must protect them from the harmful radiation in space, and from the intense heat of the Sun. They also have to return the astronauts safely to Earth. These difficulties are why the Moon is the only place in the Solar System that astronauts have visited.

The Future

A human lifetime lasts for a blink of an eye in the life of the Earth. The Earth as we know it is just a phase in its billions of years of history. The Earth was very different in the past, and it will be very different in the future. So how will it change?

Climate change

Earth's climates have been changing slowly for millions of years, and they will continue to change. There will be periods when the Earth is warmer, and periods when it is cooler. There may be more ice ages. The important question at the moment is how much our activities will affect the climate over the next few hundred years, how we can reduce these effects, and adapt to the changes.

Surface changes

The world's glaciers are slowly melting as the Earth's climate changes. They may eventually disappear altogether.

The processes that shape the Earth's surface will continue. Over millions of years the world's mountain ranges will be eroded away, and other mountains will be pushed up. The continents will gradually move from their current positions, and one day may form a giant supercontinent again.

On the other hand, the Moon will still look as does today, but perhaps with an extra crater or two. And scientists are predicting that some time in the future, the Earth will probably be hit by a large meteorite, creating a giant crater. This would destroy much of the planet's surface, cause enormous earthquakes and tsunamis, and fill the atmosphere with dust for years.

A hydrothermal vent on the ocean floor. We have only explored a tiny fraction of the ocean depths.

Earth's end

In about 5,000 million years' time the Sun will run out of fuel. It will grow into a red ball of hot gas, so large that it will swallow up the inner planets, destroying the Earth and its Moon.

Future exploration

Here on Earth, scientists are still trying to understand why tectonic plates move, and how to predict earthquakes and volcanoes. They are also trying to understand what exactly causes changes to the Earth's climates. In the future, more remote-sensing satellites will help them.

Even though we are sending space probes to the moons of other planets, there is still a great deal to find out about Earth's Moon. Several missions are planned to map the surface and study rocks and moonquakes.

Space Fact

● The Moon is slowly drifting away from the Earth by a few centimetres a year, so the Moon will look smaller in the sky in the far future. As one of the Moon's effects on the Earth is to lengthen the day, this means that days will be longer in future too.

NASA (the National Aeronautics & Space Administration) plans to send astronauts to the Moon by 2020. It is designing a new spacecraft, the Crew Exploration Vehicle, for the task. Space probes are currently looking for suitable lunar landing sites. Missions may visit the Moon's poles, where the Sun shines nearly all the time, and where there may be ice that can be melted for drinking water.

Timeline of Discovery

1609   Thomas Harriot uses a telescope to draw the first accurate map of the Moon.

1840   The first photograph of the Moon is taken.

1915   Alfred Wegener puts forward theory of plate tectonics.

1919   During a solar eclipse, it is proved that the Sun's gravity bends light slightly, as suggested by Einstein's theory of relativity.

1946   Radar is used to measure the exact distance to the Moon.

1959   *Luna 1* is the first probe to fly past the Moon.

1959   The probe *Luna 3* is the first probe to fly around the Moon. It sends back the first photographs of the far side of the Moon.

1960   The first weather satellite, TIROS 1, is launched.

1964   The first Nimbus remote-sensing satellite is launched for studying the oceans and atmosphere.

1966   *Luna 9* is the first probe to make a successful landing on the Moon.

1968   *Apollo 8* carries astronauts on their first orbit of the Moon.

This is the lunar module of the Apollo spacecraft, which carried astronauts down to the Moon's surface.

Astronaut Neil Armstrong stands on the Moon's surface.

1969   Astronauts land on the Moon for the first time aboard *Apollo 11*. Neil Armstrong becomes the first person to step onto the Moon's surface.

1970   The first lunar rover, *Lunokhod 1*, lands on the Moon.

1971   Astronauts from *Apollo 15* use a buggy to explore the Moon's surface.

1972   *Apollo 17* is the last manned mission to visit the Moon.

1972   The first Landsat satellite, *ERTS 1*, is launched to photograph and study the Earth's surface.

1998   *Lunar Prospector* orbits the Moon, and finds evidence of water ice in craters.

2004   President Bush of the USA announces a new plan to send astronauts to the Moon.

2004   The Aura satellite is launched to study the ozone layer.

Glossary

asteroid A rocky object that orbits the Sun, but that is not large enough to be a planet. Most asteroids orbit between the orbits of Mars and Jupiter.

astronaut A person who travels into space, to carry out scientific experiments, or to operate a spacecraft.

astronomer A scientist who studies planets, moons and other objects in space.

atmosphere A layer of gas that surrounds a planet or moon.

comet A small, icy object that orbits the Sun.

condense To turn from gas to liquid.

continent A large land mass on the Earth (there are currently seven continents).

crater A dish-shaped hole in the surface of a planet or moon, created by an object from space smashing into the surface.

crust The solid, outer layer of the Earth.

erosion The gradual wearing away of the landscape by the weather and flowing water.

evaporate To turn from liquid to gas.

far side The side of the Moon that faces away from Earth.

glacier A river of ice that flows slowly down from an ice-covered mountain range.

global warming The gradual warming of the Earth's atmosphere, caused by the atmosphere trapping increasing amounts of heat from the Sun.

gravity A force that attracts all objects to each other.

hydrothermal vent A place on the ocean floor where hot water emerges from rocks underneath.

lunar To do with the Moon.

meteorite A rocky particle from space that crashes into the surface of a planet or moon.

moon An object that orbits around a planet, but that is not part of a planet's rings.

near side The side of the Moon that faces Earth.

nuclear reaction When the nucleus of an atom splits apart, or loses or gains some particles.

orbit 1) Moving around the Sun or a planet; 2) The path that an object takes as it moves around the Sun or a planet.

ozone A gas that is a special form of oxygen (each particle is made up of three oxygen atoms instead of the normal two).

ozone layer A layer of ozone gas high up in the Earth's atmosphere.

planet An object in space that orbits around the Sun, but that is not part of a large group of objects, such as asteroids or comets.

probe A spacecraft launched into space to send back information about the Sun, other planets or moons.

satellite A spacecraft that orbits around the Earth.

tectonic plate One of the giant pieces that the Earth's crust is broken into.

tsunami A high-speed wave that travels across the oceans, caused by an earthquake, volcano or landslide.

water vapour The gas form of water, made when liquid water boils.

Further Information

Books

Earth (True Books)
Elaine London, Children's Press,2008

National Geographic Encyclopedia of Space
Linda K. Glover
National Geographic Society, 2005

Organizations

National Aeronautics & Space
Administration (NASA)
Organization that runs the US space
program
www.nasa.gov

International Astronomical Union (IAU)
The official world astronomy organization,
responsible for naming stars, planets,
moons and other objects in space
www.iau.org

Jet Propulsion Laboratory (JPL)
Centre responsible for NASA's robot space
probes
www.jpl.nasa.gov

European Space Agency (ESA)
Organization responsible for space flight
and exploration of European countries
www.esa.int

The Planetary Society
Organization devoted to the exploration of
the Solar System
www.planetary.org

Websites

http://earth.google.com/
Explore the Earth in three dimensions (you
need to download software from the site
before viewing the images)

http://dsc.discovery.com/guides/planetearth/
planetearth.html
Discovery Channel site about the Earth,
with interesting videos

http://www.apolloarchive.com/apollo_
gallery.html
Thousands of images of the Apollo missions
to the Moon

http://www.nasa.gov/vision/universe/
solarsystem/sun_earthday2006.html
NASA photographs and videos of solar
eclipses

http://www.keckobservatory.org/
All about the Keck telescopes in Hawaii

http://www.ucmp.berkeley.edu/geology/
tectonics.html
Animation of the movement of continents
over millions of years

Index